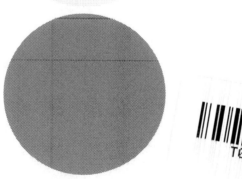

The
Pedal
on
the
Right

T0194221

The
Pedal
on
the
Right

N. M. Corcoran

Order this book online at www.trafford.com
or email orders@trafford.com

Most Trafford titles are also available at major online book retailers.

Printed in the United States of America.

ISBN: 978-1-4269-6373-5 (sc)
ISBN: 978-1-4269-6374-2 (hc)

Library of Congress Control Number: 2011905266

Trafford rev. 05/11/2011

 www.trafford.com

North America & International
toll-free: 1 888 232 4444 (USA & Canada)
phone: 250 383 6864 ♦ fax: 812 355 4082

Who?

Who is the audience for this book?

This book is rated ACRI.
Anyone can read it.

What?

*What are my hopes for anyone that reads "**The Pedal on the Right**"?*

I hope you laugh a little, and cry a little.
I hope it makes you think a little, and maybe remember your own life a little.
Then I hope that you read it again.

Where?

Where do you see this book being read?

Each chapter is a 'quick read', a story all its own. Read it anywhere, anytime.
No actual seat required.

When?

When was this book idea conceived and delivered?

TPotR was written at a River house overlooking the Allegheny River.
The delivery took one week to write, one year to 'tweak', and a lifetime to live and learn.

Why?

*Why "**The Pedal on the Right**"?*

We already have Chicken Soup for our souls –
This is the Meat & Potatoes for the other parts.

HUGS!

This book is dedicated with love and hugs to
J. J. Marlea…

You are the very best part of me;
We are the best parts of each other.

CONTENTS

Thinking Out Loud..**x**

    The Pedal on the Right 1
    …just a bit of where and why
    A Plus... 2
    …finding balance
    DUH!.. 4
    …driving lessons
    Help Yourself.. 5
    …the importance of you
    Life Destinations... 6
    …it's up to you
    No Middle Road Here.................................... 7
    …pick me – pick me!
    Shuffle Up and Deal...................................... 9
    …life's deck
    Sing Off-Key Into the Wind........................ 11
    …looking back, looking forward
    The Great Do-Over's 13
    …it is what it is
    What A Man! 15
    …bible blooper
    Where Would They Live? 17
    …medical housing

Laugh Out Loud...**19**

    Bless Me Father 20
    …holiday mishap
    Common Sense 21

...for the hearing impaired
Have Broom, Will Travel 22
...creature wars
Now You See It… 24
...vision crisis
Porcelain Virus 26
...enough is enough
So Much for the Tub 28
...who lives like this?
The One That Got Away 32
...fishing lines
Trust Me! 34
...oom-pa-pa
What Goes Around, Comes Around 35
...ladder of life
You bet! 37
...food for thought

Aches & Pain 39

Amen 40
...letting go
I Saw 41
...trust in the unknown
No One Dropped a House on Them 42
...truth or dream
Truth or Dream? 45
Super Hearts 47
...heroes among us

Love Heals 50

Angels Overlap 51
...the next frontier
Inquiring Minds Want To Know 52
...just thought I'd ask

May I Live... **53**
...grownup wish list
Sam I Am **54**
...spirit energy

Moving On **55**

I Was Just A Kid...................................... **56**
...clean slates
It Works **58**
...love that grey tape
My Choice.. **61**
...every present has a past
Today It Is! **63**
...choose your comfort zone

The Pedal on the Right

I think you can describe life as one big traffic light.
Sometimes you can fly right through it.
Sometimes you must heed the warnings and slow down.
Sometimes you just have to stop.

We will always face new paths to take.
Without warning, our lives can instantly turn on a dime.
Some turns will give us just cause for hyper ventilation.
Either way, we need direction.

In the end it all comes down to you.
Choose a destination.
Take a deep breath.
Turn the key.

Want to just sit and idle for awhile?
It might be a good day to just wait a bit and get your bearings.
You must decide.
Are you ready to go for it?

It's the pedal on the right.

A Plus

I spent many early mornings watching child-friendly cartoons with my children. We loved Dusty's Treehouse. He told simple stories with simple puppets. The messages were huge. One morning the storyline involved a small princess, who only existed to be perfect. She traveled from doctor to doctor to have a small blemish removed from her face. Each time she was advised that nothing perfect in this world can exist. Not to be discouraged, the princess finally convinced a doctor to remove her flaw. Once finished, she gazed in the mirror and stated that now she *was* truly perfect. And she disappeared.

I never cared for the "P" word, as my friends who know me well will testify. That whole 'be perfect' concept is way more pressure than we need. Instead, I have found my comfortable nest in the Minus/Plus zone. I have learned to play an easier game.

Today's headlines may be full of negativity and sadness. I choose to bless the world that is still around me, and my loved ones that woke up in it. My stomach may be growling and I have to trudge on down to the kitchen to fix the problem. What a blessing to find food to eat. The backyard bird feeder may be running empty, but the blue jays are screaming to the others to come and eat while the getting's still good! The dogs have left me a present on the sidewalk that needs scooped. Reality check – they left it *outside*! Minus/Plus.

I overheard a woman in the store complaining that she was about to be a grandmother, *again*. She was hoping that her children would stop, commenting that she had had enough. I wanted to hit her. I wanted to scream about her minus attitude and the plus of that new child to be. Instead, I took a deep breath and made myself focus on the great sale I had found on a dinner dress, and my equally pleasant salesperson. Minus/Plus.

No huge issues are needed to find this balance. Keep it simple. Smile at a stranger. Be a plus by saying hello to the person sitting in the wheelchair by the door, waiting for their special transportation. Let someone out in traffic before you. It may cost you seconds, but it may gain them a plus. Smile at yourself. It may bring you a major sense of accomplishment. Do it for you. It only takes a second to play the game.

Face the bad. Ignoring it won't make it better, but dwelling on it is destructive. Try quickly to make a choice to follow it up with something good, no matter how small or trivial. Your heart will thank you. Your friends will thank you. Your world just may be a better place.

Dessert after meals is the perfect truth. It signals the end of the moment. It leaves a good taste in your mouth. It makes you feel full.

End your moments on a good note.

Fill up with a plus.

DUH!

Okay – I understand the HUGE difference in teaching methods for men's and women's driving school.

Women's school teaches that when approaching a STOP sign:
>Remove your foot from the gas
>Begin breaking to a final stop
>Count to three, look in all directions, and then proceed.

Men's school teaches to:
>See STOP sign
>Push harder on gas; fly to within 2 feet of said sign.
>Slam on breaks.
>*Since no obstacle has physically stopped your vehicle, immediately accelerate, preferably leaving tire squeal and dust.

Driving schools will come and go, and techniques will continue to differ. So be it. Live and learn. I vote that ONE concept will and should remain without question.

If this sign is <u>facing you</u>:

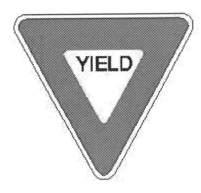

THE OTHER GUY GOES FIRST.

DUH!

Help Yourself

New Year's Eve brings promises of great change. People are known to dress in their 'make the world a better place' cloak and make solid promises of self betterment. Go for it. Any attempt, even a minute, at self improvement is a good thing.

I don't even try for anything new. I have stuck with the same resolution for years, my choice always being 'to make at least five people laugh a day'.

Sound simple? Try it sometime. You may already be doing it without realizing it, or are you making people as miserable as you are? I guess it depends on the day.

People need to laugh. Or smile. Or just feel good for a minute or two. So I tried the 'five people a day' rule. Most days it's way easy to accomplish. I don't mind being a fool of sorts. I do find humor in most things.

When I lost my dad in 1992, it was a struggle. Dark days bring dark moods. I remember riding in the final procession to the gravesite and hearing people *laughing* as we passed a local shopping area. I wondered how they could just keep on living when my world had stopped. It didn't make sense. Nor did the '5 people' rule. Like I said, I guess it just depends on the day.

Another New Year has come and gone. My resolution still remains the same. Life can kick me in the butt, but I still cling to the fact that *I* need to laugh, every single day. If someone else laughs with me – it's twice as good. Anyone is welcome to try it. Pick five people today and go for it. It may not always be easy, but you will make a difference - to yourself and to many others. It really does help.

Help yourself.

Life Destinations

Stop ~ Breathe ~ Live

Stop this minute by standing still. The world will
    continue to turn without you…promise!
Breathe this minute, slow and deep. Listen to all
    that has not stopped.
Live **this minute. It is yours. The next minute
will find you all by itself.**

Wishing you quiet moments as you discover…
    Life Destinations

No Middle Road Here

May the great toilet paper battle rage on! It is a great distraction. I'm an over towards the front person. I have ruthlessly changed rolls around in my friends' homes. They have returned the favor in mine. It's a good thing to find nonsense moments; it helps to balance out all of the serious ones.

So goes the real vs. artificial Christmas tree syndrome. I grew up with real trees. We would all vie for the coveted watering the tree position. This job was *never* to be taken lightly, and was inevitably wrapped up tight with the 'If you don't water the tree it could catch on fire' speech. The slightest screw up could cost you your entire present pile, not to mention your home. I think the tree fear factor may have forced a few unauthorized feedings by wanting to be helpful hands. I suspect some tree angel that looked an awful lot like my dad must have wiped up the extra water piles while he bit his tongue really hard.

I stayed with the real tree façade long after I had my own children. I continued the tree-watering rule with equal importance. I find it funny how the idea that I was plugging in something sitting in water never dawned on me as odd. I did have my tree epiphany one late July. Shag carpets were big in the 70's. They were actually sold with rakes to help maintain them. It didn't help.

There I was, doing something barefoot in my living room. I know that lone pine needle must have been lying in wait, getting stronger and stronger with every passing day. It was safe in the shag trenches. What had been born to a soft pine life had taken on a coat of armor. It had petrified over the last 7 months. It had embedded itself in my big toe, and held its ground. I know I yelped. I probably cried for awhile. Betrayal is a hard emotion to live with, regardless of the source. Traditions are equally hard to end. That was the day I 'crossed over'.

I have accumulated a nursery of artificial trees in my attic. Every couple of years the manufacturers make them bigger and better and easier to assemble. This wonder tree can be born again every thanksgiving and return quietly, without mess, to the attic. Artificial trees are alive and well in my comfort zone. I know the battle will continue on. You either love them or hate them. Just like the toilet paper is either over or under.

Choose your side!

No middle road here.

Shuffle Up and Deal

Children come with their very own playing cards. Life is the dealer.

No one ever mentioned to me the basic rules of motherhood. It's pretty simple. If you don't eat your young, you have to raise them. I didn't eat my young. I am still learning about that raising thing.

It was good to discover the 'cards'. They do help to cover the big events in life. What child doesn't want to use the coveted 'Birthday Party' card? They must survive their 'Kindergarten', 'Grade School' and 'First Dance' card. The 'First Kiss' card is a keeper. Best to include the 'High School Graduation card'. This is hopefully followed by the all important 'College or Trade School' card. Somewhere in these rapid growth years, parents must face the overwhelming "I need to borrow the car' card, and the inevitable 'The scratch isn't all that big' card.

Both of my children shuffled their youth decks wildly, prompting the 'You Better Call Your Lawyer' cards. If all goes well, young adults will soon choose to play their 'Get a Good Job' card, thus paving the way for the 'Move Out of the House' card.

We can only hope that our children will use only one 'Holy Matrimony' card. Not exactly dealing with a full deck, my daughter's first marriage was quickly followed by the 'Divorce' card. Brenda reshuffled her deck, quickly showing her 'Wild Card'. She remarried, and this second union involved a stepchild. She called frequently with questions concerning the 'Living with a Teenager' card.

Our son's death wrecked havoc on our worlds, including her second marriage. Brenda then played her 'All about me' card. She earned her master's degree in counseling, moved into her own apartment, got her finances in order and rediscovered her. She has since met the love of her life, and we will celebrate (with our 'Grandparents card') their new baby in the spring.

If the circle of life continues, our children will watch their children play the hands that they are dealt. How fitting. How logical.

Don't like the odds? Talk to the dealer. In the end it all comes down to

Shuffle Up and Deal.

Sing Off-Key Into the Wind

I'm amazed at life. I'm amazed at any new birth. I'm also amazed at how these new, innocent children will ever survive. Every generation has most likely looked at the newest and thought the same. We've all compared, and we're all convinced that we had it so much better.

We did.

We had tire swings that transformed energetic kids into Tarzan and Jane, or Peter Pan and Captain Hook. Or just lazy swinging in the summer sun & singing off-key to whatever wondered into our minds.

We were free to point a pretend gun formed from tiny fingers and play Cowboys and Indians without fear of being terrorists or being expelled from school.

We had penny candy that really did cost a penny. We could walk forever to the nearest store to purchase it without fear of kidnapping, molestation or 'time outs'.

We could line up, dress up and have parades in our basements to entertain the smiling parents that would sit and cheer our efforts. They would applaud the buckets on our heads, old sheet capes on our backs and broomstick batons. Any bathrobe would be an instant uniform. And any small baby could be fastened in a knapsack to an older child's back and become the Indian's papoose.

All animals that met with untimely deaths were honored with long marches around the home grounds before being laid to rest in the fields. All were covered with wildflowers and markers. All would fade into memory, but we learned at young ages about letting go.

Our cribs and playpens were probably not lead proof. Seatbelts were not regulated and flying over bumps in the road was a prime source for massive giggles.

Adult phrases were taken literally. I remember being scared to death and praying profusely in the car from a night travel with my family. My father had said that looking at the headlights from other cars could blind you. I remember it being a long drive home. I couldn't imagine daddy not being able to drive if he were blind. I know I figured it out eventually, but fear factors were different then.

May every new birth bring a new miracle of hope to this planet. May every child continue to come with the message that God is not yet discouraged of man. May they learn that buckets on their heads, old bathrobes and homemade parades can be a good thing.

May they be blessed to find a tire swing, and sing off-key into the wind.

The Great Do-Over's

It's hard for me to understand devastation by nature. Not because I don't watch the news and see the pictures. Not because I live a privileged life. I live in Pennsylvania. We have bad storms and microbursts. We survive winter blizzards and wear t-shirts that proudly display this fact. I know of one good tornado touchdown in my lifetime. My children and I sat in the dark with flashlights playing cards while the storm raged outside. We didn't even know until the next day that there was a tornado. We did drive through the area that had been hit. I know I was overwhelmed by the uprooting of trees and misplaced homes. Time and new construction have erased the physical evidence of that angry weather day. All that remains now are the pictures in my mind.

I recently traveled to Cozumel, a repeat January vacation for me. One year prior I had walked the long concrete pier, and dangled my feet over the edge. I sat for hours in that spot over the course of a week, feeding the fish & having conversations with scuba divers as they would emerge from their shallow dives. Some brought me seashells. Some would just display items that they had found lying on the bottom, before releasing them back to their watery graves.

In 2005, Hurricane Wilma shook up this world. Restaurant manager Alberto told us how they had stayed with the guests, with no way in or no way out. This raging storm covered them for three days and three nights. He filled up when he described walking through his hometown with his wife and child after the storm. He said that she had cried. I suspect that he had cried too.

I stood and looked at the spot where that long pier had been. The power of the wind and rain was overwhelming. The pier and lights and chairs were gone. How could that be? Nature had moved a concrete mountain.

The walkways are now new, as are the paint and the thatched roofs of the outdoor pavilion. They are rebuilding the outdoor cooking area, used for the fiestas. Some units have new doors and furniture. Tons of concrete and sand have made new and strong what was once old and familiar. It is all done with a great pride, as the photographs of smiling faces on the wall record the rebirth.

I am not a scuba diver like my husband, or this dive group that we travel with. I have tried this labor-intensive sport, only to realize that it takes a passion far greater than any I could give to it. Other divers have tried to encourage me to share their love. I quietly explain that taking a sometimes emotionally unstable person under water 100 feet and giving her a knife is probably not a good idea. My husband John agrees with that logic. My interests are different than his, but passion is passion, so I do understand their 'urge to submerge'. I look forward to their stories of the magical underworld that they explore.

This time it was different. The divers spoke of the newness of once familiar and sometimes staged scenery. The underwater displays were gone. Duane talked of how the sands had shifted and uncovered a whole new world to photograph. The divers were comparing the fish they had seen. Jeanne spoke of a 5 ft. spotted manta ray, a true storm survivor from the age and size. I was taken most by the baby angel fish that she described, *baby* being the key word. Such is the circle of life. Nature will always find a way.

Healing isn't always about the parts we can see.

God bless the spirit to survive, in man and in nature.

Bless our ability to cope with the great Do-Over's.

What A Man!

Okay, I know that Hollywood has its own bag of magic tricks. Such is the blessing of good set designers. I want to creep back in time to just before all of the techno happenings, and movies were made to actually play in theatres for weeks and weeks. Does anyone else find it strange that we really have no need to swarm the cinema anymore? Give it a week and you can catch the bargain Super Saver show. Better yet, buy the DVD within the month.

What's up with that?

I'm giving you all a big push back in time. If you were not blessed to even remember this Hollywood epic – you can still rent it! It is worth the trip.

Okay, Cecil B. Demille has filmed the classic epic "Ten Commandments". (You must fast forward to the end of the first disk, right before intermission.) Charlton Heston (Moses) is in the desert, looking up at the thundering mountain, home to the mysterious 'He who has no name'. Moses, his wife and half-dead friend are commenting about smoke coming from the mountain top.
"That light on the mountainside. Do you see that strange fire?" Moses asks.
"A bush that burns?" Joshua asks.
"No, it is on fire but the bush does not burn," Moses answers.
(This has all been observed from the *base* of this huge rock formation).

Okay, some logic still remains up to this point. One could see the burning bush from the ground as long as it remained in your line of vision, right? And if one could see it, it couldn't be all that far away. One would think.

Moses proceeds up the mountain with his staff. The next minute is footage of an incredible climb, up, up and away, hanging on to the

15

barest of terrain, with pain and suffering apparent from every angle and *finally* (whew!) he reaches the somewhat flat mountain top and walks *inward* to the burning bush. One can only imagine the *hours* that have passed with this journey.

Okay, Cecil created sensationalism to the max. I can accept the parting of the Red Sea. I worried for the horses trapped underwater. I cowered from the heat of the wall of spinning fire. I can accept and appreciate what was created on that massive set. But this is where I draw the line.

To this very day, I cannot help but *rewind* that mountain scene. Let's digest the moment.

"Look, Moses - see that burning bush from where you stand? It should only be a short trek if you leave right now. That's right, leave the wife in charge of the sheep and the half-dead friend. Grab that staff and go boy! Okay, judging from the sun, you've been climbing forever. Oh please be careful climbing that mountainside! You can do it! Whew! You've made it to the top! All that burning, desert sun was no match for you. No way! Now, walk *inward* to that fire bush. (Anyone notice the view of the valley? Okay, so there isn't really one). Now talk to the still-burning bush. Oh, and don't forget to wave to the people that are still standing at the bottom. If you could see that bush from where you started out, surely they can still see you now! Wave, Moses, wave! Maybe throw in a 'Hi Mom!'"

Damn, he never waves. They never show the bottom, or his wife and half dead friend. Good one, Cecil…only in the movies!

So chill your drink, pop your popcorn and go enjoy this movie.

What a man!

Where Would They Live?

I remember sitting in 10th grade science class. It was the beginning of the new school year. Our teacher was psyching us up for a class science project. We all shouted projects of choice. My friend Karen, who later did end up following her nursing dream, stated matter-of-factly, 'Let's find a cure for cancer!'

Boy, were we excited! 10th grade seems like such a big, mysterious, anything-is-possible world at 16. What our teacher had in mind was dissecting frogs and growing mold in test tubes. To bad. Maybe we could have made a difference if given the chance.

That class was in 1968. 42 years ago.

My husband and I have a construction business. We build new homes. I have been wrapped up in this adventure with him for 30 some years. The principle is basically the same for most new homes. The simple version of homebuilding 101 is: The buyer brings you money to start his home, you build a little. He brings you more money, and more of the home is done, and so on and so on until completion.

Okay – let's do a little reverse thinking here. There must be a warehouse of information and statistics somewhere that contains a really good guesstimate of the amount of money donated for cancer research since 1968. In all fairness, we have been given the great and mighty Chemo Wrecking Ball. You know, totally slam the patient's body with a poison solution and hope to wreck the cancer? The fairground circus happy person in me applauds this discovery. The real life skeptic in me asks - is this all you've got?

Follow me on this. We, the people, hand a bunch of money to a bunch of scientists to 'build' a cure for the cancer house. They work and toil and work and toil. They shuffle paper. We, the people, return with more funds so that the cancer house research continues, and so on and so on for 42 plus years.

I have just one simple question.....IS THE HOUSE DONE YET?

Or is there just more money in being sick? .

Jonas Salk opened the doors to a polio-free world by finishing his Polio Vaccine House before politics ruled positive outcome. The world *deserves* more finished developments like his.

Food for thought.

If the medical researcher's (and all others involved in the payment of the research funds) *personal* homes were built at the same rate as the medical cure 'homes'– would they tolerate it taking so long? Would anyone be satisfied to wait 42+ years for their homes to be complete?

Where would they live?

Laugh

Out

Loud

Bless Me Father

I've always admired the wooden Christmas displays that I see quietly lit in front yards over the holidays. How majestic. How heart warming. That set was on my wish list.

My sister-in-law knew of my desire to create my own wooden wonder. She sent the catalog one late September. Several large sheets of plywood, a stack of patterns and one jigsaw later, I was off and running. The set took over a month to create. We did a trial-run out in the yard just to see what the overall effect would be. My husband, John, walked down our driveway and stood below near the road to view the large display. He yelled up "Where are the shepherds?" Darn, he noticed. Having already cut, sanded and painted thirteen pieces, I was hoping to be done. I calmly yelled back, "they're in Jamaica." No good. I got back to work and added the two shepherds. The group was complete.

We decided to do the actual display over Thanksgiving. It took a great deal of effort and planning to set up the Nativity. All of the main characters had to be viewed from the road. The camels and cows and sheep had to be positioned just right. The ground lighting had to illuminate the entire scene. It only seemed fitting to also allow a space for our 100 lb. black Labrador Retriever to settle in on the straw. We were almost done!

Just as we were hanging the last piece, the telephone rang. It was my mom. She asked what we were doing. I told her that we were decorating for the holidays and that John was screwing the Angel of the Lord.....

She hung up.

I finally got her back on the line. I guess I should have said that he was *attaching* the Angel of the Lord to the house. Live and learn.

Bless me father...

Common Sense

I never shared my father's obsession with the weather. I was always satisfied to let my eyes and body do the forecasting.

If I walked outside and didn't get wet, it wasn't raining. I had the same experience with sun, snow, hail and wind. No big crackling sounds? Good. No lightning. To this very day, although I attempt to listen to the days forecast, I still rely on basic common sense. If it smells like a skunk, it's probably a skunk.

With that said, you can appreciate the fact that my entire childhood I learned to fear the dreaded 'windshield factor'. I could never understand the newscaster's obsession with such a dumb thing. Even my parents talked about it. And their problem was…? Just dig that stupid plastic scraper from out of the trunk, or behind the driver's seat, and scrape the windshield off. Why did people have to dwell so much on such a stupid issue? Never did quite get it.

Somewhere in my very, *very* late 30's, I was blessed with either a weather brain- cell miracle or better hearing. I'm thinking that since having children increases a mother's ability to hear *everything*, this is probably the best explanation.

One day, there it was! The dreaded wind*shield* factor had mysteriously become the even more dreaded wind *chill* factor. This meant dressing in twice as many layers and maybe even adding extra socks to today's wardrobe. But didn't I already know that?

Okay – you done laughing?

So I failed weather school. I'm good at other things.

Like common sense.

Have Broom, Will Travel

For the most part, I'm at peace with nature. I detest bees of any kind and leave a great perimeter for anything with claws.

I make a point of circling my home after the last snow each spring. I address all creatures, large and small, that the outside is theirs to do with as they please. The inside is OFF LIMITS. Any attempt to cross that line is cause for instant termination. Some bugs just don't get it.

Of course, I do make exceptions.

If it's a good day, I may make the noble attempt to 'Dixie cup' that wayward spider and release it back to the great outdoors. They do have a purpose…if it's a good day.

I have been known to swat at the same fly until it's no longer recognizable. I will stare at this smashed spot on the swatter and wait for any sign of life. Then I'll re-swat it again, several times, just for good measure. Bees get it even worse. My house walls will echo with my screaming 'hi-chows' as I struggle with nature to save my inside world.

I had a bird fly in once. Not a good thing. When my winged wonder finally managed to set down in an upstairs hallway, I excitedly pointed to it, hoping to enlist the help of my cat. I think Miss Kitty weighed the calm, huddled bird against my crazed, pointing madwoman antics and decided to just nap elsewhere.

Eventually the bird did manage to move to a downstairs sunroom. I closed off any chance of escape behind me and bravely shut myself into the same space. The bird did land on the top of the ceiling fan. Okay – I was tempted to turn on the fan. But what if it had a family? What if the babies would starve if this little bird died? What if I turned the ceiling fan on *high*? Instead, I opted to open one glass door. The rush of fresh air just *might* have been the welcome escape route that dumb bird needed after all. I'd like to think it was my frantic broom waving while I continually shouted "Go to the light! Go to the light"!

Have broom, will travel.

Now You See It...

Okay – what's with the eye change that mysteriously occurs when the body time clock chimes 40? I don't remember anyone warning me about this as a child. It must have fit into the sacred 'wait till you're older' category.

I've worn glasses since 8th grade. I finally graduated to contacts. Lasik surgery followed. I did enjoy the freedom of a no-glasses world for about two seconds. Before I knew it, I needed reading glasses. I think I was swallowed by the black hole of vision, forever to live with a glass framed face.

Late summer breeds fruit flies. They don't even need the encouragement of week-old bananas to find you. I think they just need air. And my kitchen.

I was doing some kitchen thing yesterday. That's when I saw that tiny black shadow out of the corner of my eye. I searched. There it was again. Let the fruit fly wars begin!

There it is. No, wait. Where did it go? Okay. Body at 2 o'clock. Slap hands together in air. Did I get it? Is that a spot on my hands? Wait – I've got to hold my hand out in front of me as I try to lean back at the same time. I still can't make out the details. I'm still too close to my own body.

Find glasses. Check hand for bug body. Missed it.

Try to find it again, wait – too blurry. Oh, I need to remove the glasses. Okay – look hard….THERE it is. Repeat air hand slap. Did I get it? Squint. Get glasses. Check hand. Repeat stupid bug war trick 5 more times.

Shut windows, set off bug bomb, exit home.

Leave glasses inside.

Now you see it…

Porcelain Virus

Fear tactics worked with kids from my era. We didn't know any better. We didn't question what adults said. Kid's rights meant a roof over your head and food on the table. Clothes came with or without new labels. Not doing well in school the first time around was not an option. Adults knew best. To question them meant punishment of the worst kind. Like cleaning your room. Or walking the dog. Or minding your kid bothers or sisters. Without pay.

My mom was an adult. My grandmother was an adult. They knew best.

I spent my entire childhood and a few of my young adult years hating public toilets. Adult legend had it that if you *ever* sit on the actual seat or if your butt *touches* any part of that seat...........

What?

I honestly didn't know what would happen if I sat on a public toilet seat. But I knew it was bad. Or would be bad. Or something might fall off.

I just figured that boys had their own scary bathroom boogie men. Something bad would happen if they didn't put the seat down after they lifted it up at home. So there must be something even worse in the public bathroom!

Like I said, if an adult said it, it was true. No questions.

I do know that other women must share this problem. It has become more than obvious over the years that others before me are still trying to master the grand toilet seat straddle. Some may have actually figured out how to *raise* the seat before attempting this ungraceful act of relieving themselves. I fear, from the evidence that most just stand and let it rip. Maybe if the adults hadn't made us stand in the first place, we wouldn't be dripping on the seat? (Am I actually questioning an adult unwritten law?)

I honestly believe that I have met thousands of people over the years. NO ONE, I repeat NO ONE has ever admitted to actually catching something unmentionable from sitting on a toilet seat. NO ONE. Not even an adult.

Therefore, to all of my scary *older adult* predecessors, please *sit* and repeat after me:

I will no longer force my insanity upon unsuspecting children. And if I even attempt this stupidity, may they have smarter parents who will put their fears to rest. Because I am stuck in my ways, I will continue to make a splash on the public toilet seats. I understand that my old bladder can no longer wait until I figure out how to cover the seat with a hundred small pieces of toilet paper. My arthritis makes it almost impossible to release and install those ready-made paper seat covers. If dripping occurs, I will not clean it off, because that will require 'contact' and maybe some scary disease that I can not afford to catch. What would my friends think? Therefore, I shall, in my old age, either remain upright and righteous, or I will learn to sit on that seat without fear or mess. My butt will *not* fall off if I use the seat that was invented for just that purpose.

So much for the Porcelain Virus.

So Much for the Tub

Remission is a welcome and painful health event. Getting nerves and muscles and other body parts back into some kind of normal is a process. Hopefully, the outcome is positive and the journey fades to memory.

I had just finished a strong dose of steroids to treat my multiple sclerosis and my dead right side. The meds had started their slow crawl through my nerve endings. I could move my toe. I was beating the odds one more time, and I would celebrate remission soon. Everyday was an improvement.

I studied my walker propped against the wall. I mentally buried it underground and hope it stays there forever. My leg was moving. My balance was returning. My gaze traveled to our outside deck. I thought of soaking for a few minutes in our new hot tub. I needed a little piece of quiet heaven.

I changed into a bathing suit, grabbed a towel and knocked on the study door. My husband looked up. I asked if he could just help me into the tub.
"I'd like to try out the new spa for twenty minutes or so…can you just help me get in"?

John met me at the tub. Just twenty minutes to soak would be so nice….

I then got a detailed explanation of the proper way to lift the attached cover. CHECK! I scooted over the edge and lowered myself into the warm, quiet water. Wonderful.

"That seat in the corner is the lounger. It's the one that I use. You can put your feet up and massage your neck...."

"This seat is fine, thank you. I just want to sit for 15 minutes or so....."

"Let me put up the umbrella. It's raining a little bit...."

"It's not really necessary, it's a light rain...it actually feels good...."

"That's why we have an umbrella. You just release this and turn this handle and-
AWWWWWW
Did you see that? That scared the hell out of me...."

A tiny, sleep-filled bat had been comfortably nesting inside the umbrella. Opening the umbrella caused the bat to drop to the spa cover. I watched it take flight at the last second. Magnificent creature.

"The umbrella is nice. Thank you. I do wish that the bat would have eaten those wasps...I pointed to a new nest, also inside of the umbrella.

"I'll get it – don't worry...

"It's okay – I'm just going to sit here for ten minutes or so...."

John proceeded to knock the bees and nest into the water. I sit in the corner of the tub watching this angry clump drifting towards me. John swept it out and smashed it into the deck.

Okay, just ten minutes......

"These are your jet controls. See that button by you arm? That's an infrared; use this control to change the lights and the waterfall. See the colors? Watch, I'll make them green...."

"I don't need the lights on, it's broad daylight. I'd like to just close my eyes and soak for ten minutes or so....."

"How about music? I can turn the stereo on. The speakers are built in. What station do you want?"

"Quiet is nice. You don't need to do that...thanks anyway...."

I sit back into the corner and close my eyes. I listen to the trees and the wind and the water moving slowly around me....

"R-E-S-P-E-C-T – find out what you mean to me" ....

What the?

"How's that. You like this station. It isn't too loud, is it? I'll be in the office if you need me...

I wait through four loud commercials until the coast is clear. I swing my legs over the edge of the tub, slip quietly inside and turn the radio down. I then return to the spa.

Sit back – close your eyes for five minutes.....I'll just rest for five minutes...

WHOOSH!!!!!!!!!!!!

What the?

A large body has just decided to join my spa interlude.

"Check out these jets. They really get the water moving! What happened to the music?

"I turned it down. I didn't care for that station...

Out he jumps to choose another station.

"It's really nice quiet" ....

"SWEET HOME ALABAMA".......

Return to the water splash...

"Hey, check this out. It's a mini vacuum. You just squeeze it underwater and it picks up debris on the bottom. Here – try it.....

"Not right now"...

Just three minutes. I'll be happy with three minutes...

"Ihaveanotherspongethatyoujustfloatinthewateranditsoaksupall theextraoilsit'scalledaduckspongeitwillhelptokeepthewatercleaning betweenchanges....

If I close my eyes and ears...

PLOP!

The dog's tennis ball has landed in the water. It drifts lazily to my corner. Our black lab Chloe wants to play fetch...my mind timer is sounding.

Just 20 more seconds and I'm outta here.....

So Much for the Tub.

The One That Got Away

It's inevitable; eventually everyone will have a fishing story of one kind or another. I am no exception.

My husband and I were blessed to find a camp of sorts along the Allegheny River. It was a great getaway for our kids. It was in a great little community with equally great neighbors. Lloyd had grown up in the area, and was what I considered the resident fishing, boating, and river expert. He was in charge of my fishing lessons.

One early July morning, we headed upriver in search of that perfect catch. As we anchored right off shore, we heard a rustling in the nearby grasses. The first noise is ignored. The second got our attention. The third was moving toward us, and it was an animal with some weight behind it.

Lloyd stated very matter of fact that it could be a bear. Well, be still my heart. How scary and exciting at the same time. We readied to start the boat motor just in case, and waited, very silent.

There it was again – the mysterious form would take shape any second!

The grasses parted, the body moved quickly towards us and entered the water. SLAP. Its' tail sent a spray of water into the air and off it went. It was a big old beaver. What seemed a lumbering heavy body on land was now a gracefully swift creature in the water.

We couldn't contain ourselves! Lloyd figured it to be at least 30 pounds. He was like a kid at Christmas. He said in all his years on the river that beaver was definitely the largest one he had ever seen. We sat for several minutes in total amazement at what we had just witnessed. So much for fishing. We pulled anchor, and headed back to camp. I know he was anxious to tell the others about it.

Halfway home, I turned around in the boat and faced him. He slowed the motor. I said I needed to talk to him for a minute. He stopped the engine.

I said "Lloyd, I know how exciting this was, and how much you want to tell everyone about what we saw. But I'd really appreciate it if, when you talk about it, you don't use my name in the same sentence with it."
He looked at me strangely. He didn't quite get it.
I took a breath. I said "Lloyd – DO NOT SAY - I went fishing with Nanci today and saw the biggest beaver I've ever seen."

I thought he might fall out of the boat.

And then there was the one that got away.....

Trust Me!

I think polkas should be mandatory at weddings. A good DJ will crank that bass sound and fill the hall with oom-pa-pas! How fitting (and kind) for all us older & wiser guests. Some will never know the importance of the polka. Raspberries to you!

Ever notice that no 'older' guest will ever complain about how loud the polka is?

Let's all try a bit of honesty for a moment. Even the most *proper* figure will cut one on the dance floor during a polka. Talk about a blast from the past. You've just consumed rich, processed, over-seasoned foods that you seldom ever eat. You've toasted the happy couple and clinked away at your glasses of far from top shelf alcohol. You've applauded the bridal dance and other fun hoopla that goes along with this happy occasion.

You've delayed your visit to the bathroom.

Finally – the base resounds and you jump at the chance to be up off of your chair. Then the garlic moment hits you. Thank you Mr. D.J.! You welcome the chance to oom-pa-pa right along. Every other heavy step down to the beat brings another toot.

All of this is done without fear or shame of any recognition. After all, who could possibly know it was you? By the time the telltale aroma hits one's nostrils, you are way clear of the evidence. Blame it on the next guy! How wonderfully perfect!

Ever wonder what the dance floor might sound like if the music suddenly stopped? A regular dance floor symphony beyond all symphonies… one great ballroom blast!

Keep the polkas. It's the best good time we older folks have on the dance floor. It's our salvation.

Trust me!

What Goes Around, Comes Around

I compare the age categories of life to one big ladder. We evolve through our *Newborn* (demanding, helpless, diaper, baby food world) to *Pre-teen* (Pre-PMS, somewhat respectful). We vault to *Teenager* (Free spirit, knows everything, never wrong), freefalling through *Young Adult* (con artists with boobs or testicles). We leap to *Adult* (self supporting, somewhat educated and hopefully employed) and glide gracefully to *Older Adult* (set in their ways and stubborn because they damn well earned it).

The older I get, the more it is evident that once up the 'ladder', the only logical path is to go down the other side.

The 'growing up' levels from Newborn to Young Adult are pretty much controlled by the Adults. Stay in bounds. Follow the rules. Know what is socially correct. Yada, yada.

I'm thinking that we get the big 'free pass' if we make it to Older Adult and start sliding down the ladder backwards. How wonderfully free to just let go after a lifetime of rules. You *did* damn well earn it!

The irony is that Older Adults on the downward spiral are untouchable. They can officially discard the 'could a, should a, would a' handbook. It's called paybacks!

My mom is in the downward spiral. After a lifetime of 'proper', by the rules, and 14 children, she's just living life on her terms.

Recently, we went out to lunch. Once done, we drove to the local mall for her to spend a gift certificate, again. Why is nothing right once it is tried on at home, and must be returned to the same store over and over?

We had entered the department store at ground level and walked thru the aisle to the escalators. Since I still possess the gift of walking more than 5mph, I stepped onto the moving stairway before mom started her ascent. I turned to acknowledge her, and noticed a gentleman also getting on behind her. Mom loudly announced "Boy - am I gassy" and proceeded to prove her point.   Being the understanding, concerned adult daughter - I quickly faced forward and doubled my steps to the top. There I sought shelter in the closest department with the tallest displays.   To this day, my heart bleeds for the poor gentleman that, once started up the escalator behind her, was totally committed to finish out the ride.

Wait a minute. What is this? Could this really be? This same woman who preached and lived socially acceptable was throwing all caution to the wind! She was just living. How positive. How grand.

I guess the age thing really is about what goes up, must come down.

This is also fair warning to my daughter; though she does assure me that good drugs and a nursing home are my best bet.

Who knew?

What goes around, comes around.

You bet!

I was vacuuming and noticed that elusive penny. You know - the one that causes a flash of brain movement - 'Pick it up, sweep it up? Pick it up, sweep it up?

Penny candy being a thing of the way past – I let the sweeper do its thing.

I hear the rattle through the hose, and the final quiet as the copper menace settles into the dust bag. Good – no clogs in the hose if the penny rattled through.

Since vacuuming is a no-brainer – and not wishing to have a totally clueless day, I search for a brilliant analogy.

CORN! I have discovered the purpose of corn!

We salivate over the typewriter fashion that we inhale that early summer delight. We steam the frozen gems throughout the year. We butter, we salt, we enjoy - and then…we find it the next morning after the coffee has kicked in. There it is, in all its glory - 'floating' evidence of the meal the night before.

As you are either gagging at this thought or having that reserved chuckle – the truth is – there is a reason! Think about it. Just like the penny rattling through the sweeper hose – so have those kernels taken on that huge, magical voyage. They have survived the stomach acids, the intestines (both large and small) and lord knows what other road-blocks in between.

The point is – it has emerged into the final resting place – the porcelain 'dust bag' if you please.

No clogs – no blockage! Maybe your body just handed you (well, not literally) a somewhat clean bill of health.

So continue your munching frenzy, it really is a good thing! But will you ever eat this sun colored veggie without thinking of this story? Doubt it.

Will you *look* for the after evidence next time you indulge, just to be sure?

You bet!

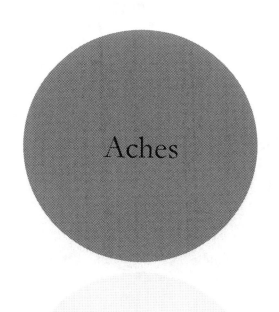

Aches

and

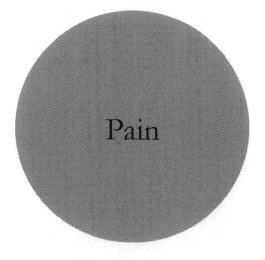

Pain

Amen.

As I visited with my friend Annabelle, I questioned the strange choosing of life and death. Why her? Why this wonderful, gentle soul? The cancer was winning the war, as it raged through her tiny frame.

Today's headlines screamed with terrorists and war; of spills and crashes. I picture the 'grand master' of life just shuffling up the deck of the day. Whose picture card would be turned and played today?

I sat and held this phenomenal woman's hand and remembered a palm reader of long ago. "You're a healer," she said. I had choked on her words.
"Then why couldn't I save my dad?" I had cried.
"Only you can answer that," was her reply.

A decade later, I sit and ask the same question. Why can't I heal this woman? All I can do is visit and hold her hand. WHY?

As I walked the quiet river road to my own home, there it was. The answer was inside of me all along.

'Healing isn't always about the parts we can see.'

One month later she was gone. Three months after that, two of our close friends were both blessed with baby girls. My world can celebrate two brand new Annabelle's. How perfect is the circle of life.

'Healing isn't always about the parts we can see.'

Amen.

I Saw

We all handle the passing of a loved one differently. We will look and listen for signs that they may still be among us. We look for signs that they have crossed over. We talk to ourselves and we talk to the air, making believe we have a chance of any answer in return.

It's my way of helping me, and your way of helping you. We convince ourselves that we just might have…but not really…but you never know…because just maybe…but chances are …

It's all good.

I looked for you.

I looked for you in the heavens, and you showed me white clouds and blue skies.

I looked for you in the stars, and you showed me Orion.

I looked for you in the trees; you showed me colorful birds calling out to the world.

I looked for you in the grasses; you showed me a great buck resting until dusk.

I looked for you by your grave; you showed me twin butterflies spinning around.

I looked for you in the wind, and you took my breath away.

I looked for you.

I saw.

No One Dropped a House on Them

'No parent should have to bury a child'.   I heard that phrase a lot growing up. Older friends, TV stars, books. It's just something you hear other people say.

My sister Teri had lost her son, Jared, in 1994. He was 94 days old. The autopsy report said SIDS. I know it was sad. I wrote his eulogy poem. The priests talked on and on about how Jared was an angel. I watched Teri and her husband Dan carry that tiny white casket down the aisle at church. I wondered how she would ever survive this. Her world had stopped. Life went on for the rest of us.

I thought back to the birth of my own son in 1973. I sat holding this newborn baby wondering, if given the choice, what great wish gift I would make for him. Perhaps no hurts, no broken bones or broken hearts? Success? Money? No disease or illness? The possibilities were endless, in a perfect world. Reality check, mom. I made my choice.

"Please let my child die fast doing something he loves".

He did. He was.

October 9, 2003 I received the 'call that no parent should ever get'. My son had died in Idaho where he was base jumping from the Perrine Bridge. Jason loved skydiving. He had logged over 2000 jumps and almost 200 base jumps, which are jumps from a fixed point, usually involving a short but calculated distance. He was an exceptional instructor. He had phenomenal body control. He was getting married the following July. Jason had just turned 30. The death certificate read "Blunt force trauma". This wasn't happening.

I thought of my sister Teri and her son nine years prior. I wondered how I was going to survive this. The world had dropped a house on me.

I know that I functioned for the first year. People still needed me, and I still needed to deal with my anger issues.

I finally had a shouting match with THE MAN. I wanted answers. I can't imagine any stronger bond or greater need than a mother for her child.
WHY MY SON?

It took almost a year before the Idaho police released the parachute that Jason had used when he died. First I just sat beside the box. Then I opened it slowly, giving my emotions time to ground. I dressed in his vest – the unwrapped chute and strings trailing behind. I cocooned in it. I cried. I hit my knees. I *screamed*. WHY MY SON?

Somewhere in that fleeting moment between rage and calm, I listened. And I got an answer. It came like a whisper, and wrapped ever so tight around me…
'*Because I needed him more'.*

That wasn't fair. God needed Jason - pure and simple. Jason died fast doing what he loved. It was the gift wish I had made for him at birth. He didn't suffer. He wasn't left a paralyzed quad in a chair wired with feeding tubes. He wasn't a mangled body that would have hated to be alive. God took him fast and left him whole. I hate it - but I have to love it. It really is quite brilliant.

And the world kept turning.

One day I looked in the bathroom mirror and saw this person staring back at me. I wondered where she'd been for the last year or so. I guess its all part of that grieving, healing thing. I felt like I was just waking up from a long, restless dream. I know that I had pulled away from those closest to me. I know the thought of also losing them was overwhelming. I know my true friends hung in there with me. My husband never pushed for more, but allowed the space that I needed to just breathe. I know that he needed the same space. He was stuck under a house too. I did get a puppy to test my heart strings on. It seemed logical in my world.

Instead of celebrating Jason's marriage the following July, we took a family trip to St. Lucia. I needed a different kind of memory for that month. I sat under a palm umbrella on that sandy island and felt something erupt inside of me. I bummed a paper and pen. I scribbled:

Truth or Dream?

Urgent, urgent.
Must return the call. "There's been an accident. He didn't make it…"

Truth or Dream?

Ring, Ring.
Answer the phone. "Hi Mom, is Dad there?"

Truth or Dream?

Knock, knock.
Delivery to the door. "You have so much mail, did someone die?" Small chuckle for the unthinkable.

Truth or Dream?

Snip, snip.
30-year-old lock of hair locked behind a 30-year-old baby picture.

Truth or Dream?

Dig, dig.
Cold form, dark space, fresh dirt.

Truth or Dream?

Rows and rows of 'Thank You' notes. Thank you for sharing the worst moment of my life, for flowers and food and cards. Thank you for one more awful job to do. This is etiquette?

Truth or Dream?

Tick, tock.
Buried heart. Yours for sure; mine too, I fear.

Truth.

I will never look at a peace lily again and not cringe. I am now thankfully aware of the 'lost year' time gap. I will gladly share this insight with anyone that needs it. I will tell them to find their own safe space, and wait. Your heart will wake up. You *will* laugh more and cry less. Your dreams will get better.

I have gotten to know the names of those long-gone at the cemetery buried around my son. I have introduced myself to them. I still cry when I'm alone. I still breathe. Time still remains my best friend.

It's good to cherish one or two close friends that will accept your mood swings no matter what. People do go on with their lives, even though yours seems at times to have stopped. It doesn't make them cold or unfeeling. They still care about you. They just function in their own world. And that really is okay.

No one dropped a house on them.

Super Hearts

My childhood heroes were Peter Pan and the Lone Ranger; Superman and Mighty Mouse. All magical beings, all out of reach to us mere mortals.

With cinema technology, they've only become bigger and better. Good. Who doesn't need a hero or two sometime in their lives?

Funny, it took sitting in the hospital with my dying father to see the hero that he was. How many others have touched my life? Friends, relatives, even strangers? My mailperson, Julie, gives that extra effort to bring packages to my door, instead of leaving them at the curb. My refuse collector leaves the emptied can standing upright, instead of down where it can roll into the street. I watched an elderly man use a cane to steady himself while he held the door open for a mom pushing a baby stroller. And can we bless the hard-working people that make my water safe to drink? Ditto my car serviceman. Every day people. Funny how none of them wear capes or masks or possess magical powers. Or do they? Maybe if costumes were required, it would be easier to recognize the heroes around us.

It took one hero's death and writing his eulogy to set me on my path of hero discovery. This man was a simple, educated, giving soul. He stayed faithful and married to the same woman for 44 years and raised 14 children with her. He loved life. He made a difference. I'd like for you to meet him.

Dear Dad,

    As I sat with you in the hospital, I wondered how I would describe you to someone who had never met you.

I would have to tell them of your gentle ways and firm hand, your quick smile and silent strength, your love for your country and your flag, of music and home movies and sports and train whistles...of sunrises and sunsets.

I would tell them of how you had given a lifetime to being both teacher and student, husband and father, brother and friend.

I would tell them of your passion for travel that took you to all of our United States except Hawaii – and flew you a world away to Germany.

And I would say that you helped to shape the lives around you as meticulously as you planned your trips.

If there were trip-tics to heaven, you would have planned that trip too. You would know the exact mileage to heaven (going 3 different routes, of course). You would plot every rest stop (15 minutes only) and you would know every road hazard and speed trap. You'd know what parts to avoid, and what parts were worth seeing. You'd know the exact time of departure and would do everything possible to arrive on time. And you'd call ahead your reservation months in advance.

I would say how you loved and guided each of your children, helping them to plan the 'trip-tics' that would take them through their own lives.

I would say how you gave all of us roots – strong bonds to home and family, a respect for life and country and a love of nature and good friends.

And then I would tell how you'd given us wings. And when it came time for each of us to try our wings, you and mom hugged us goodbye and then hugged each other as we took flight; ready to catch us if we fell, but forever the 'wind beneath our wings'.

How do you describe a man who has been bigger than life with a heart to match?

You once said, "You can worry about dying tomorrow, or you can live today...take your pick". You always lived today, and you always lived it your way.

Goodbye Daddy...we love you...we will miss you. Be safe now. Be free.

My father didn't wear a cape. He didn't jump tall buildings in a single bound. Neither can the doctors, nurses, dentists, teachers and bus drivers in my world. Nor the cashiers, secretaries, stock persons and yes, even your parents or guardians. They will dress like everyone else. They cannot reflect bullets of hate. They bleed. They hurt. They cry. You'll know them by the one super power that they do share.

They all have super hearts.

Angels Overlap

Ideas come from life experiences. Death steals family members and friends from us. I need to believe that I will see my stolen Angels again...

They are all familiar faces
That have gone ahead to wait,
To comfort when our time has come
And bring us closer to the gate

They smile with wonder and with love
They've walked this path before
And now they hold us near to them
As they lead us thru the door

For this is where we're meant to be
To heed our final call
To guide our restless spirits home
And catch us if we fall

Take comfort in this final act
Of leaving old for new
Trust in your long last leap of faith
There's nothing more to do

As they have gathered long before
Their wings so gently wrap
So we shall join and fall in line
When our Angels overlap.

Inquiring Minds Want To Know

I have a question.

When people ask "Is there life after death"?
Are they referring to the one who has died?
Or the one that is left behind?

Inquiring minds want to know.

May I Live

A favorite game of youth was playing 'Mother May I?' Those that do remember playing and asking the question, may also remember waiting with childhood apprehension for the 'Yes You May!' answer. It may have inspired this grownup version…

May I live to change you,
>	and celebrate as I watch you change.

May I live to read you nursery rhymes of twinkling stars,
>	and celebrate as you discover the solar system.

May I live to introduce you to words,
>	and celebrate as you grow in knowledge.

May I live to sing to you,
>	and celebrate when music touches your soul.

May I live to buy you crayons,
>	and celebrate the rainbows of your life.

May I live to surprise you,
>	and celebrate as you discover new directions.

May I live to love you,
>	and celebrate as you share your heart unconditionally.

May I live to see you live?

Sam I Am

Long before 'spiritual guide' was an understood term, I lived with unexplained influence. I had a 'drive' of sorts, giving me direction and ideas; a whispering in my dreams.

My childhood was labeled as 'creative'. That was easy to accept. But I knew things. When I announced at the age of 6 that my mother was going to have twins – everyone smiled and patted me on the head. Since my mother wasn't even privy to such info, that just could not be. Smile, smile…pat, pat. My dad woke us that late august morning and said that mommy had had the babies. She had delivered twins! So there!

It wasn't until my thirties that I started questioning physic phenomenon and the unexplained happenings around me. The thought of other forces helping to guide us became very real to me. By my forties, my force had a name. Not knowing if this energy was male or female, I chose Sam. It seemed appropriate. I have learned to ask Sam directly for help. I know that Sam is helping to guide this book. Am I creative? Lots of people are. Why? Maybe we've just learned to listen a little better. You never know where the big ideas are going to come from.

Thus my belief that we are all restless spirits left over from someone else's lifetime. I believe that we are all dealt the good and bad hand at birth. I believe that our job, for however long we have, is to make the good and bad better. What we improve goes with us, the unimproved staying behind for the next body to correct. Or not.

My wish? To be given the chance to be a 'Sam'. To maybe be good enough to help someone else realize the potential in their own dreams, to be a 'whisperer' of sorts. I also pray for that one brief, mystical moment in the end - for the chance to approach the entity that has been my guide in this world and crossed me gently into the next, and have them say

Sam I Am.

Moving

on

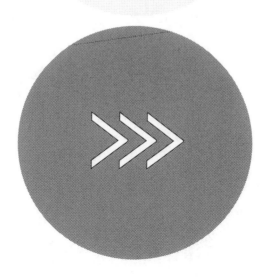

I Was Just A Kid…..

If we can survive our own childhood, we can probably survive anything.

Being raised in a large Catholic family, our nightly ritual involved hitting our knees (as a group) and petitioning the saints and angels to prepare our souls for whatever that night may bring.

Catholic guilt ran rampant through our veins. Most big families stuck together; exchanging clothes, large quantity recipes, and new discipline measures. Spy networks were formed, so any attempt to wear a touch of ninth grade makeup or dress just a little in style (having now entered the world of – OH MY GOD! – PUBLIC school) was reported back to some mom and immediately sent over the mommy panic party lines.

No talents were encouraged, nor after school activities. Being a mommy before you were a mommy was the after school activity. Want to stay for basketball? WALK home since mom was busy with the other dozen kids where *you* were expected to be. College? Yeah right. The boys were made to join the service if they wished for a college education. (The government would help pay for it.) Girls were sent out looking for the coveted secretary positions – preferably along a bus line, as no transportation would be afforded.

I had been accepted at Art school. School loan? Heaven forbid! We were being raised by the LCFVP. (Remember that crap about 'it takes a village…' – we were blessed with the Large Catholic Family Village People) We were instructed to work first and save the money for college, then we would be able to continue our educations. Most of us dated fast and married young to escape the big family syndrome. Most of us had babies right away. What other world did we know?

Have regrets? Who doesn't? I lived for years with the inward panic of all of the stupid stuff I had done growing up. I would relive walking down the hallways at school and being excited about the sudden boy attention, only to realize that my button was opened on my blouse and my whiter than white bra was showing. Years later, my daughter's music professor laughed with her about the day her mom fell off of the music stand backwards, chair and all.

I had accumulated a mental overstuffed closet of stupid kid moves.

It took me 40 yrs to realize I could let it go. The closet cleaning was long overdue. I forgave myself and anyone else for the black memories. I've even laughed at a few, once I dusted off the black. All that I was, and all that I lived was what made me the person I am today. Would Art school have changed that? Would better clothes or more money or a smaller family? It just doesn't matter. It ALL made me strong. The nasty, abusive nuns. The hand-me-down clothes. The daily church masses, even Saturdays – that was confession day. The horrid sheltered embarrassment of high school. (What did those swear words mean???) The funny whispered comments of teachers and schoolmates about what caused my big family. *I* didn't even know what caused it until a friend whispered it to me in study hall.

All the childhood crap. And that was what it was – CHILDhood crap. If I could change anything about my early school days, I would choose to go back and form a 'club' of sorts that included anyone who didn't belong anywhere else. All the other 'outcasts'. You know – the ones whose dad didn't own a car dealership, or the ones that lived in the big homes with only one other sibling. The cheerleaders and the jocks; the perfect TV families with perfect clothes and perfect teeth. Just picture it! An honest to God 'come as *you* are' club. I'd like to think that it might have helped us to belong. Maybe not. Bet our membership would have been bigger than the 'perfect kids' group.

Whatever. I did survive. And for the first time, I was able to just let it go. Why? I finally gave myself permission to color outside the lines. I gave myself permission to accept exactly what I was!

I was just a kid..............

It Works

Eighteen was a strange year. I graduated from high school. I landed the coveted secretary job with a finance company downtown. I was discovering my wings.

I went numb.

I learned quickly that medical doctors are not God. They weigh the odds. They give us their best shot. When in doubt, they use words like 'psychosomatic'. Physical Therapists are all about exercise and strengthening. They compare notes with the medical doctors. They stick together. Chiropractors are x-ray lovers and long term weekly caregivers. Parents are just hoping for an answer to make it better. All are good in their own right.

Almost one year from its start, the numbness in my body left. The medical doctor credited a lesser need for attention. The physical therapist credited my exercise. The chiropractor credited cracking me the right way. My parents' prayers were answered.

I married and had my children. We were building a house. I continued to live with dead limbs off and on, not wishing to return to my previous doctors. I lived with this for nine more years.

My sister, Judi, had had enough. Working in the medical field, she called one day with the date and time I was to see a neurologist. I met with this giant of a man. Dr. Wachs asked me questions. He did a few quick tests. He told me that I might have Multiple Sclerosis. He let me cry. Then we talked. To this day I believe that I cried more from relief than fear of the possible condition.

He scheduled a three day hospital stay with extensive testing. They had to rule out everything else. Guess I pulled the 'if everything else is negative, this is it' card. He told me that they were testing for spinal cancer, or a brain tumor, or brain cancer, or worse. By the third day, I was relieved to find out that it was *only* MS. I wasn't crazy. I wasn't making this up. I finally knew what was wrong with me.

Over the years, I've lost the use of every part of my body. Meds work. I have been blessed to get the broken parts back.

People ask what MS is all about? I have found that the MS 101 class works the best. I tell them to picture the floor lamp in their home. With the light plugged in, you flip a switch and the light works. Now cut the cord. You can turn that switch off and on all you like, but the signal gets blocked. It's the same with me. My nerve endings swell up and block the signal. Meds reduce the swelling, like taping the break in the cord. The signal gets through and, for a time, I work again.

My daughter Brenda once asked, in tears, if she would get MS too. I remember holding her and (almost laughing) telling her that the only part of MS that she would get would be PMS. I was (thankfully) right.

Eventually, I may be faced with a no-fix break. I'll cross that bridge when I have to. In the meantime, I have learned to rely on the strength of my family and friends. My heartfelt thanks go to the person who invented the walker. Having dogs, I do avoid putting tennis balls on the rails. But what freedom that wonderful metal contraption affords to the stubborn streak in me.

My husband John has earned hero status with the crap he's had to deal with. He never left when I needed him to stay. He willingly changes his schedule to become my taxi. He encourages me to rest. He makes it okay for me to slow down, and understands how I struggle with this backwards rule change. I hate needing anybody to help me around. Aren't I supposed to be there for everybody else? He allows my illusions of grandeur and picks up my pieces. He keeps me real.

He never quit on us, even though I gave him every reason to walk away from my broken mess.

Are you feeling a little broken? My family and friends are at their best when I am at my worst. Maybe the world works the same. Crisis brings out the humanity in all of us.

I believe that we can all use a good dose of human 'duct tape' to help fix the breaks. Go out and grab a roll. Someone you know and love may need your help.

It works.

My Choice

He was screaming in her face as he held her down.
"Keep your eyes open".
She saw his two fingers held straight out – she knew he would pull his
arm back and run those fingers into her eyes.
"This is really going to hurt" she cried.
"Keep your eyes open" he screamed.
"I can't", she cried.
"DO IT" he shouted.
The room went dark – I heard her scream.

And then I woke up.

I think I cried for three days over that dream. The woman had looked
like me, but it wasn't me. As hard as I tried to bury that memory, I kept
replaying it in my mind.

My daughter Brenda called around that third day. She knew I was
troubled. As hard as I tried to be strong, I broke down and cried as
I told her what I remembered. As a Professional Counselor, Brenda
asked questions about the dream, helping me to step back from the
situation and, using Gestalt Dream Interpretation, walked me through
it, without fear and emotion.
We concluded that I was (finally) ready to face my past with my eyes
open. Memories that I had buried deep within me – memories I
wanted desperately to forget, wanted out of the shadows.

And yes, it was going to hurt, but I had to keep my eyes open.

Ouch. Who wants to do that?

So I went on with my days, feeling better about the dream. I tried to
'bury' it – like I always did. But the door has been opened. And flashes
of childhood and family issues became alive again in my mind.

Looking back hurts. But looking with adult eyes and heart and mind can make the difference. *Every present has a past*, and for me, two questions needed to be asked. How deep is it buried? What will be the cost to exhume it?

Brenda suggested that it was okay for me to remember the events, but stressed the importance to deal with each one. Some would make me cry. Some would make me angry. Some would just be totally dumb and not worthy of any more energy. Either way, after reviewing I will place each memory in its own 'box'. I can then find a place for it on a 'mind shelf' and just leave it.

So what has changed? I looked – I faced – I conquered?
The memory will always be there tucked away. I can revisit it again at anytime - or not… but this time with my eyes open.

MY choice.

Today It Is!

Don't you just love it when people say 'If I could do it all over again.....'
Better yet – 'If I knew then what I know now..........'

Do what? Know what? Change what? What, exactly, would you repeat if you already knew the end result?

Grade School? Ouch! – Double that if you were sentenced to a Catholic school....
High School? Yeah – your skin looked so good........
Weight gains, weight loss....
Would you relive childbirth? Would you even *consider* it if you 'knew then...
DATING? Okay, maybe that first kiss.....
Sex, marriage, commitment.............
Life's lessons? Broken bones, broken hearts?
DEATH? Like flushing that goldfish wasn't traumatic enough, then you lose your family and friends?

If today you woke up breathing – you're ahead of the game.

Sure, most of us had some great times – who wouldn't want to relive them? But since that stupid phrase "If I knew then what I know now" is usually used to denote changing bad to good – I ask again. Which year would you choose to return to? If you really could 'go back', would you? Would you relive your life again?

I vote NO. I'm sticking with today. I've never been this age before. Good or bad, today it is.

Next time you roll over another year – feel blessed. Don't even complain about it. Instead, please accept this birthday wish from me to you:

Okay - it's the day after your birthday, so it's a fact!

You are OFFICIALLY still alive and on this planet.
YOU DID IT! You lived to celebrate another year of you.
How ultimately wonderful!
Celebrate all that you have, and all that you have accomplished;
All that you may have lost, but more, what you have gained.
Celebrate all that you have seen, and all that you are still here to see!
The powers that be have given you another year,
Another day,
Another minute!
Celebrate you and your next new day.

With all you have right now, would you go back? What would you choose to do?

Good or bad, today it is!